SOUND WAVES
TO MUSIC

Design	David West
	Children's Book Design
Editor	John Clark
Picture researcher	Cecilia Weston-Baker
Illustrator	Ian Moores
Consultant	Alan Morton PhD
	Science Museum, London

© Aladdin Books 1990
Designed and produced by
Aladdin Books Ltd
28 Percy Street
London W1P 9FF

First published in
Great Britain in 1990 by
Franklin Watts
96 Leonard Street
London EC2A 4RH

ISBN 0 7496 0184 1

A CIP catalogue record for this book is available from the
British Library.

Printed in Belgium

HANDS·ON·SCIENCE

SOUND WAVES TO MUSIC

Neil Ardley

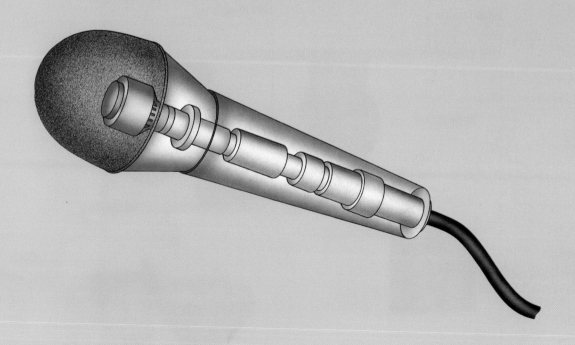

GLOUCESTER PRESS
London · New York · Toronto · Sydney

CONTENTS

This book is about sounds — from the quietest notes played on a violin to the boom made by an aircraft as it flies faster than the speed of sound. It tells you about what sound is, how sound moves, and how we hear and use sound. There are "hands on" projects for you to try, which use everyday items as equipment. There are also quizzes for fun.

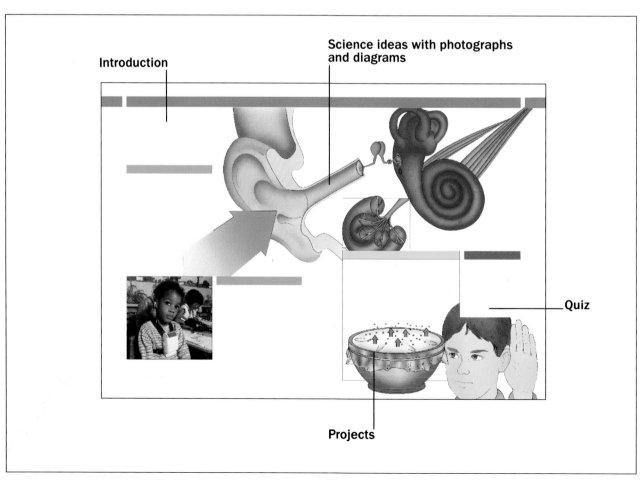

Introduction

Science ideas with photographs and diagrams

Quiz

Projects

INTRODUCTION

Sound is very important to us because we use it whenever we communicate with other people. Spoken words enable us to express and exchange ideas and information, as well as our feelings about things. Although sounds cannot travel very far by themselves, we can communicate with people around the world using sound with the aid of the telephone and radio.

Sound is also important because it gives us music. The sound of voices raised in song and instruments playing together can have a powerful emotional effect on people. We are able to listen to all kinds of music by means of the radio and sound recordings.

The recording and broadcasting of sound is a very big industry, and involves many millions of pounds. Most people have record players, tape players and radios in their homes. Many people also play some sort of musical instrument themselves.

Voices and instruments combine to make music

Things have to move to make sounds. Banging and scraping noises occur when things strike each other or rub together. A strong wind whistles through trees and howls around buildings. Moving parts inside machines make sounds. The sounds themselves move too, rushing through the air at high speed.

SHAKING WITH SOUND

Really loud noises can make things shake. Also, shaking causes sounds. Clapping your hands together disturbs the air around your hands so that this air shakes, or vibrates. The vibrations spread out through the air and reach your ears, and you hear the sound.

Most things that vibrate give out sounds. Striking a bell, for example, makes the whole bell vibrate. The vibration sets the air around the bell vibrating too, and the sound of the bell spreads out in all directions. The sound dies away as the vibration comes to a stop. Musical instruments vibrate all the time as they produce musical notes.

THE SPEED OF SOUND

When you listen to people talking, you hear their voices as soon as they move their lips. The sound seems to travel instantly from their mouths to your ears. In fact, the sound takes a short time to reach you — about a hundredth of a second from a person across a room. This time is so short that you do not notice it.

The speed of sound in air is about 330 metres per second. This is about a million times slower than the speed of light. You can therefore see things happen some distance away before you hear them — like a flash of lightning and the thunder it makes. Count the seconds between the flash and the thunder. Divide by three, and this is the distance of the flash in kilometres.

△ A drummer sets the skin on a drum vibrating as he strikes it with a stick. The skin vibrates and gives out sound.

△ The sound of thunder takes some time to travel through the air and reach you after a flash of lightning.

SPEAKING AND SINGING

Lightly touch the front of your neck while you are talking. You will be able to feel your throat vibrating. This is because you have two bands called vocal cords inside your throat. When you speak, the vocal cords vibrate and set the air in your throat and mouth vibrating. Out comes the sound of your voice.

You have to breathe out and push air through your vocal cords to make a sound. Open your mouth wide and make a sound without moving your mouth: this is the basic sound of your vocal cords. When you speak, you use muscles in your throat to control the cords, and you move your mouth and lips to vary the sound. You get different notes in singing by changing the opening in your vocal cords.

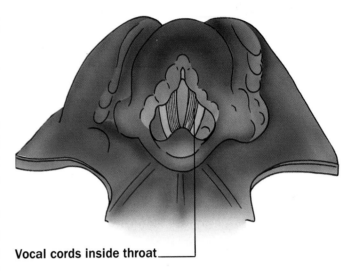

Vocal cords inside throat

▷ We make sounds as soon as we are born. But it takes years to learn how to make sounds that others can understand.

BALLOON NOISES

Blow up a balloon and stretch the neck sideways between your fingers. It makes a sound because escaping air causes the neck to vibrate. Pull hard to close the gap and you get a higher note. Loosen the neck to open the gap, and the note is lower.

Your vocal cords make sounds in much the same way as when the air vibrates in the neck of the balloon.

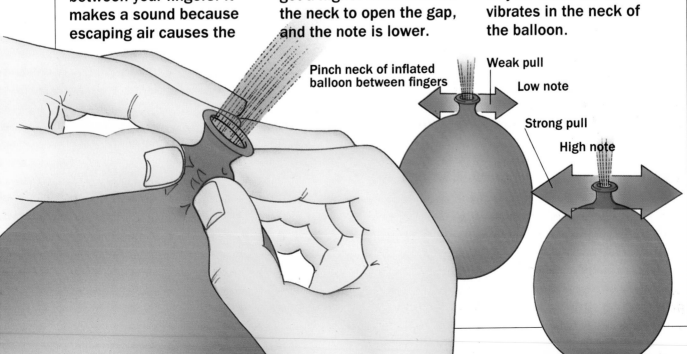

Pinch neck of inflated balloon between fingers

Weak pull

Low note

Strong pull

High note

Sound travels through the air in waves. These are not like water waves, in which the water level goes alternately high and low. A sound wave consists of alternate regions of high-pressure air and low-pressure air moving through the air. A vibrating surface pushes and pulls at the air to produce the pressure changes.

LOUD AND SOFT

When you shout to make a loud sound, you have to use a lot of effort. Being quiet and making little sound involves using little effort. The loudness or softness of a sound is called its volume. A loud sound has a high volume, and a soft sound has a low volume.

An object, such as the string on a guitar, must vibrate strongly to make a loud sound, which is why it takes more effort to vibrate it. The size of the pressure changes in the sound, or the amplitude of the sound, is greater than with a soft sound. The amplitude depends on the distance that the sound-making object moves as it vibrates.

HIGH AND LOW

Human voices and most musical instruments do not only sound loud or soft. They also produce high or low notes. These notes differ in pitch. Women and young children have high voices, whereas most men have low voices.

The pitch of a sound depends on how often the pressure of the air changes. This in turn depends on how often the object producing the sound vibrates. A string that vibrates quickly gives a high note, whereas slow vibration gives a low note. The rate of vibration is called the frequency of the sound. The wavelength of the sound, which is the distance between the pressure changes, also varies with pitch. A high sound has a shorter wavelength than a low sound.

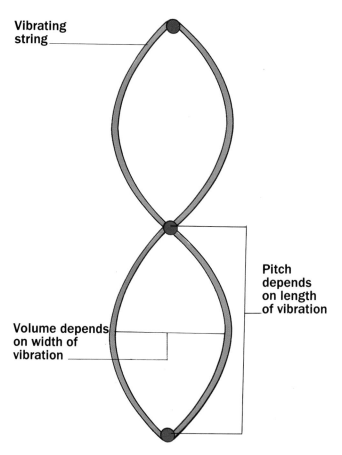

Vibrating string

Pitch depends on length of vibration

Volume depends on width of vibration

▽ The strings inside a piano have different lengths. Short strings give high or treble notes, whereas long strings give low or bass notes.

NOTES FROM A RULER

Hold a ruler over the edge of a table and twang it to make it vibrate. Hear how using more effort makes the ruler vibrate more widely and gives a louder sound. Move the ruler to lengthen or shorten the vibrating part. The vibration gets faster and the pitch rises as the vibrating part gets shorter.

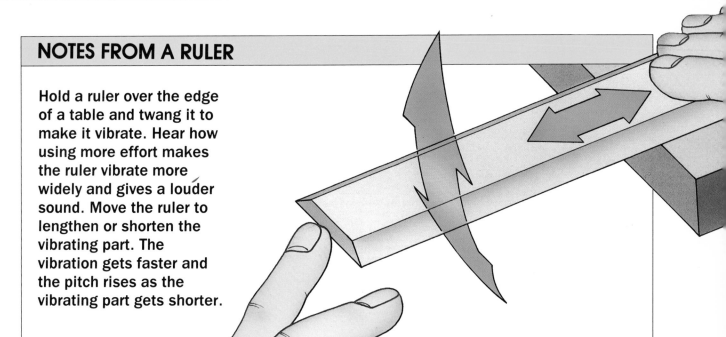

MEASURING SOUND

Loud sounds, like the roar of traffic or aircraft, can be a nuisance. They can also be dangerous. Very loud sounds can damage hearing and cause deafness. A special meter measures the loudness of sounds in units called decibels. The softest sound that a person with normal hearing can detect has a level of about 1 decibel. Sounds of 120 decibels or more can be painful.

People who work with noisy machines may have to protect their ears, because listening to loud sounds for a long time can harm their hearing. Listening to tapes with earphones can also cause damage if the sound is very loud.

△ This workman is wearing ear muffs to protect his hearing from the loud noise of the machine.

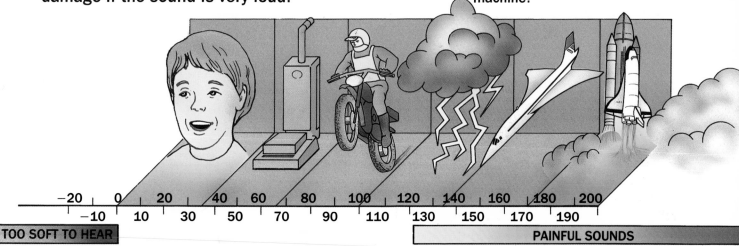

−20	0	20	40	60	80	100	120	140	160	180	200
−10	10	30	50	70	90	110	130	150	170	190	

TOO SOFT TO HEAR   PAINFUL SOUNDS

We detect sound waves passing through the air with our ears. They react to the pressure changes in the waves and we hear the sounds. Having an ear on each side of the head enables us to tell where sounds come from. We can also tell one kind of sound from another, enabling us to recognize people by their voices.

INSIDE THE EAR

Each of the lobes on the sides of our head that we call an ear is in fact only part of the ear. The rest is inside the head. The visible part is the outer ear. It collects sound waves and funnels them into a tube leading to the middle ear.

There the sound waves reach the eardrum, a small flap which is attached to several small bones. The bones link the eardrum to the cochlea in the inner ear. The eardrum vibrates as the pressure changes and the sound waves reach it. The vibrations pass to liquid inside the cochlea. This sends a signal along the auditory nerve to the brain, and we detect the sound. The semicircular canals in the ear enable us to balance.

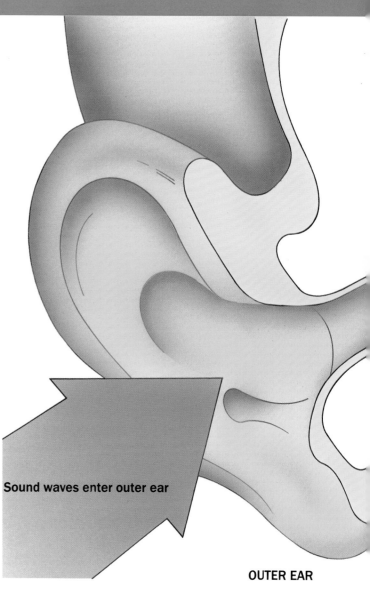

Sound waves enter outer ear

OUTER EAR

△ A deaf aid or hearing aid fits comfortably into the ear. It is rather like an earphone and makes sounds louder.

HEARING PROBLEMS

Some people cannot hear very well. Loud and clear sounds are soft or muffled, and soft sounds cannot be heard at all. This is deafness. People who are totally deaf cannot hear any sounds.

Slight deafness can happen if the tube in the outer ear gets blocked with wax. A doctor can easily clear the tube, and hearing returns to normal. A blow on the ear or very loud sound can damage the eardrum and ear bones, and diseases may affect parts of the middle ear or inner ear and cause deafness.

Placing a hearing aid in the outer ear makes sounds louder and may overcome deafness. Sometimes, an operation can be done to cure serious deafness.

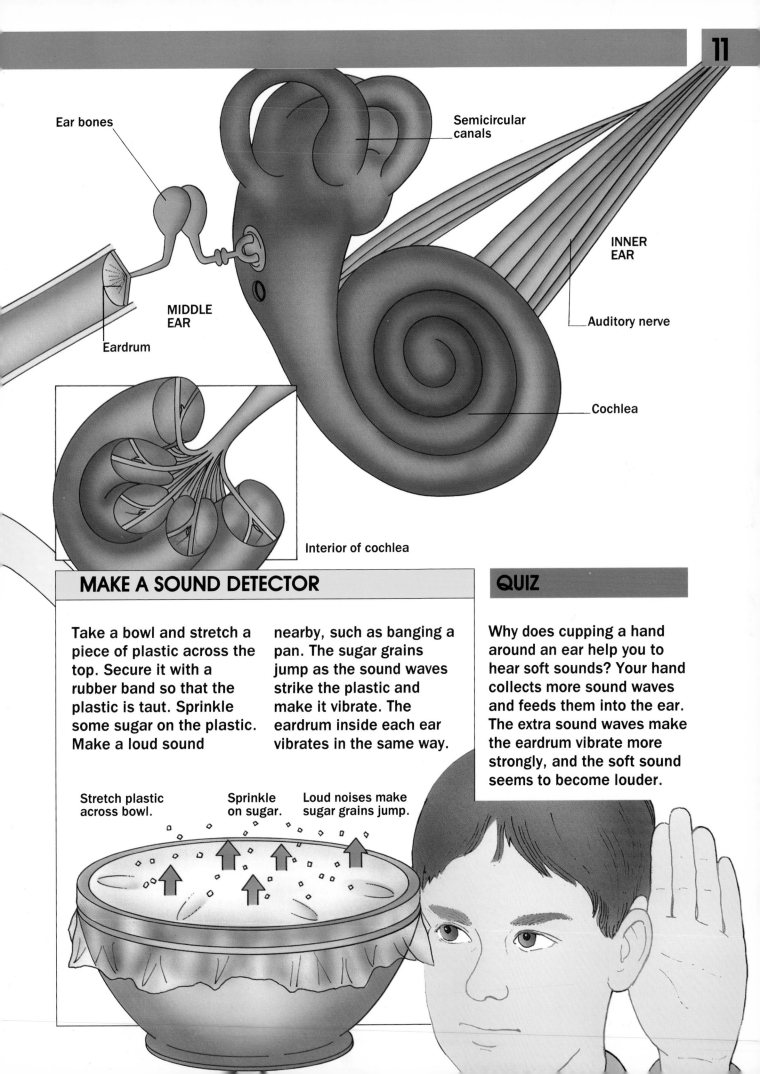

Ear bones

Semicircular canals

INNER EAR

Auditory nerve

MIDDLE EAR

Eardrum

Cochlea

Interior of cochlea

MAKE A SOUND DETECTOR

Take a bowl and stretch a piece of plastic across the top. Secure it with a rubber band so that the plastic is taut. Sprinkle some sugar on the plastic. Make a loud sound nearby, such as banging a pan. The sugar grains jump as the sound waves strike the plastic and make it vibrate. The eardrum inside each ear vibrates in the same way.

Stretch plastic across bowl.

Sprinkle on sugar.

Loud noises make sugar grains jump.

QUIZ

Why does cupping a hand around an ear help you to hear soft sounds? Your hand collects more sound waves and feeds them into the ear. The extra sound waves make the eardrum vibrate more strongly, and the soft sound seems to become louder.

Sound waves do not travel only through air. They pass through other kinds of materials. Water and hard materials can transmit sound. Sounds can penetrate walls and windows, and enter a building from outside. But some materials soak up sound, and it is possible to make a room soundproof.

PIERCING SOUNDS

All things are made of many tiny particles called molecules. When sound waves pass through a material, they make the molecules vibrate. As the molecules move together, there is a region of high pressure. They then move apart, and a region of low pressure follows.

The molecules are close together in hard materials like steel and in liquids like water. Sound travels more quickly through these materials than in air, and it travels farther too. This is why sounds come through glass windows and brick or stone walls to enter buildings.

SONIC BOOM

Supersonic aircraft such as Concorde can fly faster than the speed of sound. However, these aircraft may make a loud bang called a sonic boom as they pass overhead at supersonic speed.

Air moves out of the way as an aircraft passes, causing pressure changes that

△ Sounds travel long distances through water. Dolphins are able to communicate with each other in the sea by using sound when they are far apart.

form sound waves travelling at the speed of sound. When the aircraft moves at the speed of sound or above, a very sudden increase in air pressure occurs. This strong pressure then moves out and is heard as a bang when it reaches the ground. The boom may cause damage, so supersonic aircraft usually fly slower than the speed of sound over land.

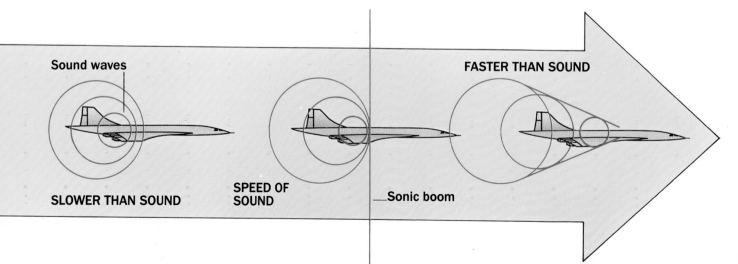

Sound waves

FASTER THAN SOUND

SLOWER THAN SOUND

SPEED OF SOUND

Sonic boom

STOPPING SOUND

Soft materials soak up sound because their molecules do not easily cause each other to vibrate when sound waves strike them. Recording studios have walls that contain soft materials to stop any sound getting in from outside.

Windows containing two panes of glass – called double glazing – cut down sounds. This is because sound does not travel through the air gap between the panes as easily as it does through glass. Silencers on cars cut out the sound of the engine. They contain materials that soak up sound, or a series of plates called baffles that block the sound.

▽ This room is lined with materials that soak up all sounds, and it is totally silent inside. It is used for testing the noise levels produced by the engines of new cars.

▷ There is no sound in space because space is totally empty. Astronauts outside a spacecraft use radio to talk to the crew of the spacecraft.

SILENT WORLD

The astronauts who went to the Moon could not talk to each other in the usual way – they had to use radios. This is because the Moon has no air. There are no molecules to transmit sound from one place to another, and so everything that happens on the Moon happens in total silence. The only way to make sound travel directly from one astronaut to another would be for them to touch helmets. Sound waves could then travel through the material of the helmets.

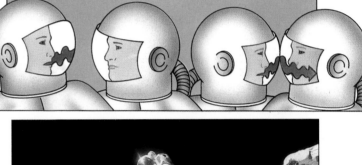
No sound travels   Sound travels

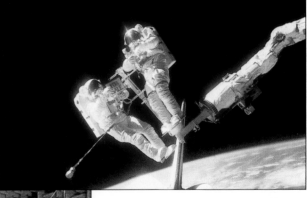

QUIZ

Tap your teeth very gently with a pencil. Why are the sounds so loud? The sound waves travel through your head to your ears without going through the air.

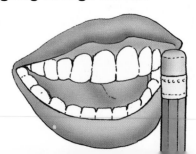

Sound waves moving through air may strike a surface, like the wall of a room. The waves bounce off a hard surface and move back into the air. Soft surfaces like curtains soak up the sound waves and the sound does not return. The way in which sounds bounce before they reach us can change the quality of sounds.

ECHOES

If you stand in front of a high wall or cliff and shout, the sound of your voice may come back to you slightly later. This is an echo. The sound waves travel from your mouth to the wall or cliff, bounce off it and return to your ears. You may hear lots of echoes in large places like cathedrals and under wide domes. The sound waves bounce around several times. The echoes lengthen the original sound so that it takes time to die away.

GOOD LISTENING

When you listen to music in a concert hall, you hear sounds bouncing from the walls and ceiling as well as the sounds coming from the stage. All these sounds mix together to give the music a good

△ Sound bounces round the Whispering Gallery at St Paul's Cathedral, London.

quality of sound. The shape of the hall and the materials on its walls and ceiling greatly affect the quality of the sound. Builders of halls have to study acoustics, which is the science of sound.

▽ The interior of a concert hall is designed to produce a good sound for the audience.

CAPTIVE SOUNDS

If you are ill, the doctor may want to listen to the sounds inside your body, such as the beating of your heart. The sounds are very soft, but the doctor can hear them with a stethoscope. This instrument has a long tube with a small, flat funnel at one end and earpieces at the other.

The doctor puts the funnel on your body. The sounds enter the funnel, which feeds them into the tube. They travel up the tube, bouncing from one side to the other. The stethoscope captures the sounds coming from the body and sends them directly to the doctor's ears. The sounds do not spread out as they would in the open air, and this makes them loud enough to hear.

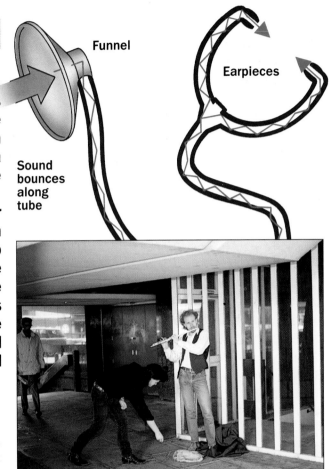

Funnel

Earpieces

Sound bounces along tube

▷ The sound of music played by buskers can bounce along the sides of passageways. This makes the sound louder than it would be outside.

TICKING TUBE

Two people take a long cardboard tube each and point it towards a wall. Each tube should be at the same angle to the wall. One person places a ticking watch at the end of one tube. The other person listens at the end of the other tube, and should be able to hear the watch ticking. Without the tubes, the watch cannot be heard.

The sound waves from the watch travel along one tube, then bounce off the wall and enter the second tube to reach the ear of the listener.

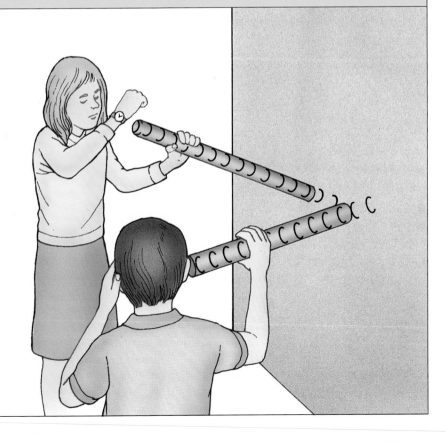

Strange as it may seem, there are lots of sounds that we cannot hear. This is not because our hearing is imperfect in any way. The sounds are too high in pitch for our ears to detect, although some animals can hear them. This kind of sound is called ultrasonic sound or ultrasound. It can be used for many purposes.

SOUND NAVIGATION

Several animals use sound rather than sight to find their way and to get their food. Bats sleep by day and feed by night. They fly about in total darkness, avoiding obstacles and capturing insects to eat. A bat emits squeaks of high-pitched sound, usually too high for people to hear. The sound waves bounce off obstacles and insects and return to the bat's large and sensitive ears. The bat is able to work out the distance and direction of obstacles and insects from the echoes it hears. This is called echo location, and high sounds work better than low sounds. Other animals, such as some whales and dolphins in the sea, also use echo location to find food and to navigate.

SONAR

Ships use beams of ultrasound to measure the depth of water, to chart the sea bed and to find shoals of fish. The system is called sonar, which stands for sound navigation and ranging. A transmitter under the ship's hull sends out regular pulses of sound. These bounce off the sea bed or shoals of fish and return to the ship. A detector picks up these echoes, and turns them into a picture on a screen or draws a chart.

The time it takes for the echoes to return depends on the depth of the sea bed or fish. Sonar measures this time and shows how deep things are. It can even show the outlines of objects such as submarines or wrecks on the sea bed.

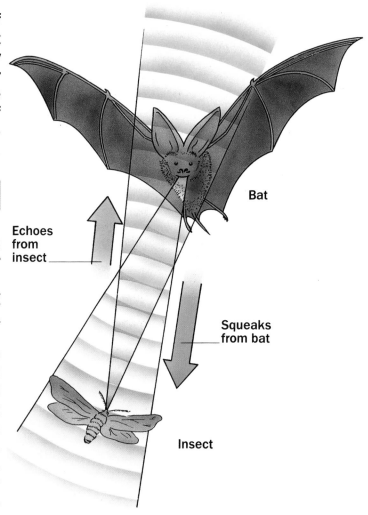

Echoes from insect

Squeaks from bat

Bat

Insect

▽ A sonar screen displays a picture of the water beneath the ship. Shoals of fish can be detected by sonar.

FIRST PICTURE

One of the most important uses of sound is the ultrasound scanner. This instrument is able to show a picture of an unborn baby inside its mother. Doctors can use the scanner to check that all is well with the baby before it is born.

The scanner works in the same way as sonar. A transmitter sends a beam of ultrasound into the mother's body. A detector then picks up echoes that come back from the baby. The beam scans the baby and builds up its picture on a screen. It seems that ultrasound scans are harmless to both mother and baby.

▷ The pictures of an unborn baby made with an ultrasound scanner show parts inside the baby's body as well as the whole baby.

SOUND AT WORK

Industry also makes good use of ultrasound. Detectors can check metal parts for internal faults such as cracks. A beam of ultrasound bounces off any faults in the metal and can reveal that the part may be about to break.

Ultrasound waves vibrate very fast — over 20,000 vibrations per second. Powerful beams of ultrasound can make materials vibrate so much that they heat up. Ultrasonic welding machines are used to weld plastic parts together.

▽ Ultrasonic detectors can test the metal of an aircraft to check for any cracks.

Music is one of the most enjoyable ways in which we use sound, whether we are performers or listeners. Two of the main groups of musical instruments are string instruments and percussion instruments. We set these instruments vibrating and making sounds basically by twanging and banging them.

STRING SOUNDS

All string instruments contain a set of stretched strings or wires. A violin and a guitar have only a few strings, whereas a piano and a harp have many. You use a bow to play the violin, while you pluck the strings of a guitar and harp with the fingers. Playing piano keys makes felt-tipped hammers strike the strings inside.

The strings respond by vibrating, but little sound comes from them. The vibrations then spread to the body of the instrument, which vibrates much more and produces the sound of the notes. The pitch of the note depends on how thick the string is, how long it is, and how tightly it is stretched.

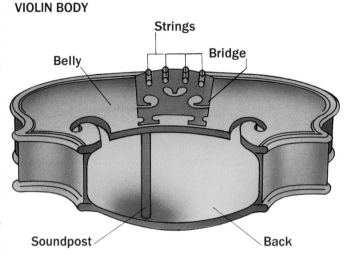

VIOLIN BODY

Strings

Belly

Bridge

Soundpost

Back

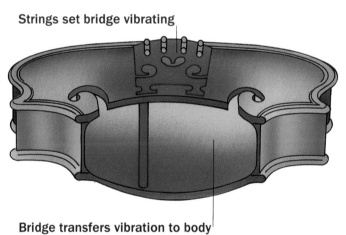

Strings set bridge vibrating

Bridge transfers vibration to body

DRUMMING

Most drums and many other percussion instruments make noises rather than notes at set pitches. You strike, shake or scrape them to get a sound. Hitting a drum with sticks or the hands sets a skin stretched tightly across the end of the drum vibrating. The air inside the drum vibrates too, and out comes the thud or boom of the drum.

Cymbals and gongs are discs of metal that vibrate to give a crashing sound. Rattles contain beads that click together. Other instruments consist of pieces of wood that you scrape or bang.

▷ A drum kit contains a set of drums and cymbals played by one person with both hands and, using pedals, both feet.

BARS AND BEATERS

Tuned percussion instruments are played with sticks or beaters to produce sets of notes. Some consist of a set of metal or wooden bars suspended on a frame, like the xylophone. Hitting a bar makes it vibrate and give out a certain note, which depends on the size of the bar. Bigger bars give lower notes. Some instruments have a set of tubes beneath the bars. The air vibrates inside a tube when the bar above it is struck, making the sound louder. Handbells and church bells contain clappers that strike the bells to set them ringing.

▷ The marimba is a kind of large xylophone that is very popular in Africa and Central America.

TEA CHEST BASS

The double bass is a big string instrument. You can make a kind of bass with a tea chest (or a large strong box), some string and a broom. Turn the tea chest upside-down and fix the string to the bottom. Rest the broom handle on the chest. Tie the other end of the string to the broom. Grip the string and pull the broom back so that the string is taut.

Plucking the string gives a deep note. Slide your hand up and down the handle or pull on the broom to get more notes.

Pull handle back and pluck string.

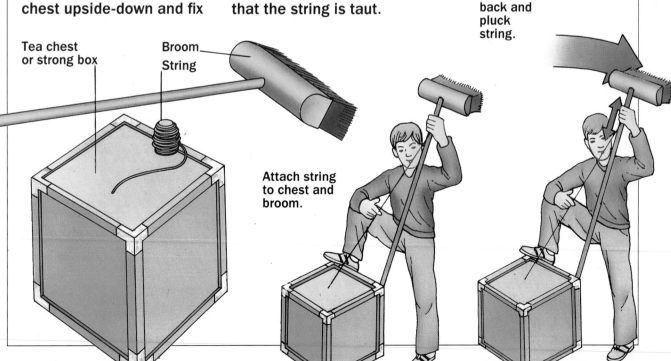

Tea chest or strong box

Broom
String

Attach string to chest and broom.

Blowing into a pipe can produce a sound as the air inside the pipe vibrates. Musical instruments that work in this way are known as wind instruments, and there are two main groups. Woodwind instruments have holes in the pipe to get different notes. Brass instruments usually have a pipe that changes length.

WHISTLES AND FLUTES

Woodwind instruments have pipes of wood or metal. There are fingerholes along the pipe, which may be closed with the fingertips or with pads pressed down by the fingers. In whistles and flutes, which include the recorder, the player blows across a hole or a sharp edge cut in the top of the pipe. This sets the air in the pipe vibrating and out comes a note. Its pitch depends on the length of the pipe from the mouth to the first open hole.

△ The rods and keys on a modern flute help the player to play more easily.

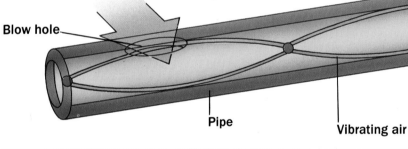

Blow hole

Pipe

Vibrating air

▽ The saxophone, created by the Belgian inventor Adolphe Sax in 1846, is widely played in jazz and popular music.

REED PIPES

Several woodwind instruments have a mouthpiece containing a reed at the top of the pipe. Blowing the mouthpiece makes the reed vibrate, and the air in the pipe vibrates to produce a sound. The clarinet and saxophone have a mouthpiece containing a single reed. The oboe and bassoon have a double reed, which is two reeds bound together.

The pipes of these instruments have different shapes. The clarinet is the same width throughout, but the other instruments are wider at the bottom than the top. The shape of the pipe and the kind of reed affect the sound and give these instruments their particular tones.

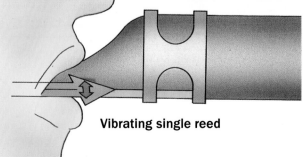

Vibrating single reed

BRASS

Brass instruments include the trumpet, trombone, tuba and various kinds of horn. They all have a long brass tube folded back on itself, with a mouthpiece shaped like a small cup or funnel. Blowing into the mouthpiece makes the air vibrate inside the tube to produce a set of a few different notes. These are the notes in a bugle call. All the other notes are made by changing the length of the tube. Making it longer gives lower notes.

The trombone has a slide that moves in and out to change the length of the tube. Other brass instruments have valves. Pressing the valves changes the length of the tube to give a different set of notes for each valve position.

▷ Pressing the piston of a valve inserts an extra piece of tubing into the tube of the instrument and lengthens the column of vibrating air inside it.

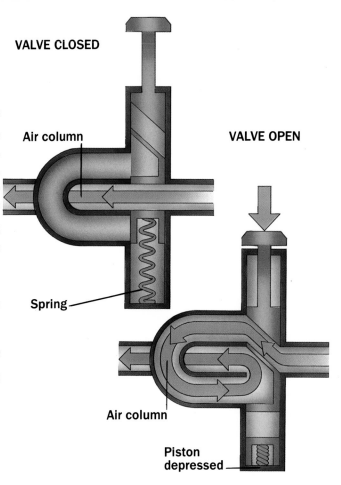

VALVE CLOSED

Air column

VALVE OPEN

Spring

Air column

Piston depressed

BOTTLE ORGAN

You can make a simple organ with a few bottles. Fill them with different amounts of water and blow across the tops of the bottles. Each one gives a different note depending on the amount of water. Adjust the water levels until you get a set of notes.

An organ has a set of pipes of different lengths that give different notes.

Each bottle is like an organ pipe. The note depends on the length of air in the bottle. Fuller bottles give higher notes because the length of air is shorter.

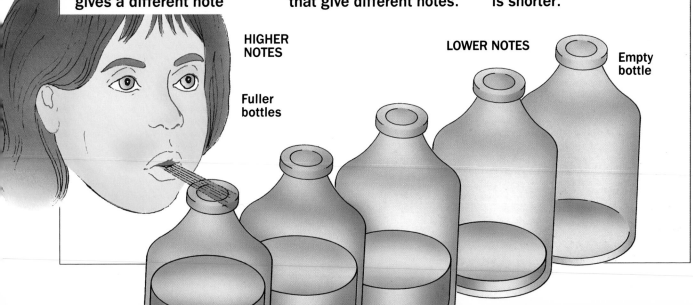

HIGHER NOTES

LOWER NOTES

Empty bottle

Fuller bottles

Our voices and musical instruments are not very loud. Speakers who have to address a large crowd need to shout. Singers and musicians cannot sing or play loudly enough to entertain the huge audiences that want to hear them. These people therefore often use sound systems to boost their voices and music.

SOUND SYSTEMS

A sound system uses the power of electricity to make sounds louder. It works by first turning the sound waves into an electric signal. The strength of this signal is then increased, or amplified, and the stronger signal is then turned back into sound waves. The sound waves are now much louder.

A microphone turns sound into an electric signal, and an amplifier strengthens the signal. A loudspeaker turns the signal back into sound.

△ Bands which perform at big concerts and festivals have powerful sound systems that make their music very loud.

ELECTRIC EARS

Singers and performers sing and play into microphones, which are rather like electric "ears". Inside each microphone is a diaphragm that vibrates as the sound waves strike it. The diaphragm is linked to a detector. This turns the vibration into an electric signal that varies at the same rate as the vibration of the sound waves.

There are several different kinds of detectors. One kind contains a small coil of wire suspended inside a magnet. As the sound enters the microphone, the coil moves to and fro in the magnet's field. This causes the coil to generate an electric signal. A cable carries the signal to the sound system, or to the transmitter at a radio station.

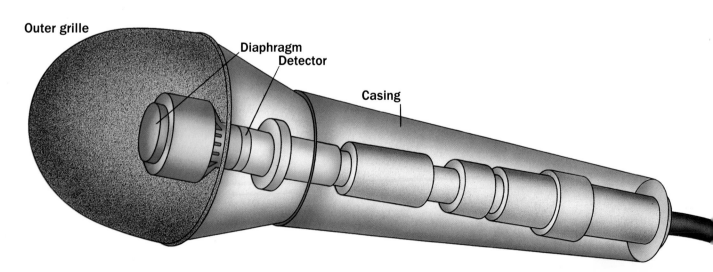

Outer grille

Diaphragm

Detector

Casing

STRENGTHENING THE SIGNALS

Microphones are often connected to a mixer in a sound system. This combines the electric signals from microphones. An engineer uses the mixer to set the final volume levels of all the sounds.

The signals from the mixer go to the amplifier, or a microphone may connect directly to the amplifier. The signals from the mixer or microphone are quite weak and go to transistors or electric valves in the amplifier. These use the weak signals to control a stronger current in the amplifier. They make the current vary at the same rate as the signals, which is the rate of vibration in the original sound. The current is turned into strong signals.

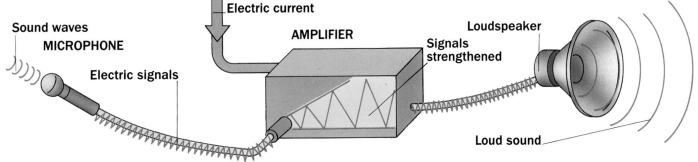

Electric current

Sound waves
MICROPHONE

Electric signals

AMPLIFIER

Loudspeaker

Signals strengthened

Loud sound

SOUND PRODUCERS

Strong signals from the amplifier go to two sets of loudspeakers placed, if it is a rock concert, on each side of the stage. The loudspeakers turn the signals back into sounds. A simple system may have just one loudspeaker.

A loudspeaker contains a moving coil and magnet like those in a moving-coil microphone, but much larger. The varying signal goes to the coil, making it vibrate. The coil is connected to a cone, which also vibrates. This vibration has the same rate as the original sound, but is much stronger. Out comes the sound at high volume. A set of loudspeakers has loudspeakers with cones of different sizes for high, mid-range and low sounds.

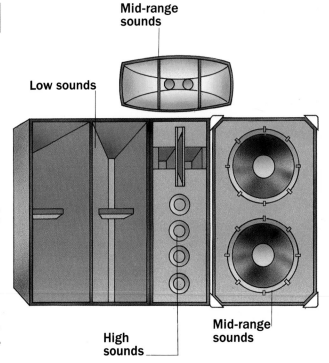

Mid-range sounds

Low sounds

High sounds

Mid-range sounds

Many of the musical instruments that people play are electric instruments. These include the electric guitar and synthesizer. An electric instrument itself makes little or no actual sound when it is played. Instead, it produces an electric signal, which goes to an amplifier and loudspeaker to give the sound.

WIRING THE GUITAR

The electric guitar and the bass guitar, which is a kind of electric guitar, both have strings and are played like an acoustic (non-electric) guitar. Beneath the strings, which are made of metal, are one or more pick-ups. The pick-up produces an electric signal that varies at the same rate as the strings vibrate. It contains a coil of wire wound around a magnet or set of magnets. The vibrating string makes the magnetic field vary, which generates a varying electric signal in the coil. The signal goes along a wire to an amplifier and loudspeaker, and out comes the sound. Controls can change the volume and tone of the sound.

△ The electric guitar was invented to make the guitar louder. However, the instrument now has a sound all of its own.

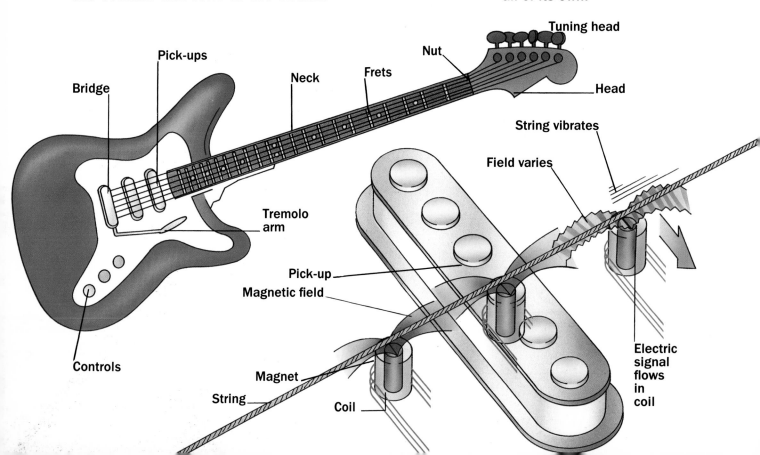

Tuning head

Pick-ups

Bridge

Neck

Frets

Nut

Head

String vibrates

Field varies

Tremolo arm

Pick-up

Magnetic field

Electric signal flows in coil

Controls

Magnet

String

Coil

MUSIC MACHINES

Most synthesizers have keyboards and are played in a similar way to the piano or organ. Other synthesizers can be played like a guitar, wind instrument or drum. All contain electronic parts that generate an electric signal when the synthesizer is played. The signal goes to an amplifier and loudspeaker to produce a sound.

A synthesizer can produce many different sounds. These may be the sounds of musical instruments or totally new sounds. The controls on the synthesizer can change the kind of signal that is generated by the electronic components to get different sounds. A sound sampler is a similar kind of machine that can store any sound in the form of an electric signal and then use it.

▽ Although this synthesizer looks like an organ, it can sound very like other kinds of instrument — or even an orchestra.

COMPUTER CONTROL

The kind of music made by synthesizers is sometimes called electronic music. A small computer can be included, connected to a synthesizer and sampler. The computer can store notes played on the synthesizer in the form of electric signals. It can then send the signals back to the synthesizer to produce the music. The computer is able to correct any mistakes that were made in the playing. A home computer and synthesizer can be connected to a stereo system to make electronic music.

QUIZ

How many musicians make the music that you hear on films, television and radio? Often it is only one person using a computer and synthesizer to produce all the different sounds.

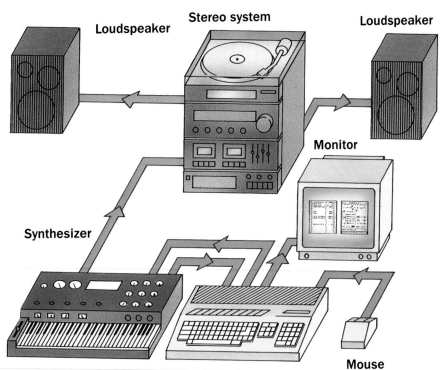

Loudspeaker Stereo system Loudspeaker

Monitor

Synthesizer

Mouse

Computer

Sounds come into our homes from distant places when we listen to the radio. We can speak with others almost anywhere on the telephone. Electricity, radio waves or light rays carry the sounds. These travel so fast that the sounds reach us almost instantly, and we can talk with people as if they were next to us.

TALKING TO ALL

When someone calls you on the telephone, a microphone in their mouthpiece converts the sound of their voice into an electric signal. This travels to the earpiece of your telephone, which contains a small loudspeaker to change the signal back into sound. The sound may travel along wires as a coded electrical signal, or it may be changed into a radio signal that moves through the air or a light signal travelling along glass fibres. The signal is directed through telephone exchanges that connect the two telephones together.

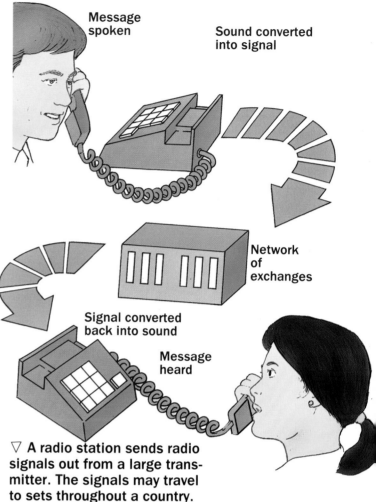

Message spoken

Sound converted into signal

Network of exchanges

Signal converted back into sound

Message heard

TUNING IN

A radio receives sound in the form of signals from a radio station. Microphones at the station turn the voices or music into an electric signal. This signal is then changed into radio waves that vary at the same rate as the vibration of the sound waves. There are two kinds of waves: AM (amplitude modulation) and FM (frequency modulation), meaning that either the amplitude or the frequency (and wavelength) of the radio waves varies. The radio receiver changes the radio signal into an electric signal, which a loudspeaker changes into sound.

▽ A radio station sends radio signals out from a large transmitter. The signals may travel to sets throughout a country.

Amplitude

Wavelength

AM (amplitude modulation)

FM (frequency modulation)

Sound wave

SOUNDS ON THE MOVE

Radio enables people to contact each other when they are on the move. Vehicles such as taxis and police cars have radio sets and transmitters so that drivers can talk to their headquarters. There are also radios called walkie-talkies that people can carry. CB (Citizens' Band) radio is used by drivers to talk to each other over short distances.

Many people have portable telephones that they can use wherever they are. These work by radio, which links the telephone to a network of radio stations that are part of the telephone network.

▷ A police officer uses a portable radio to talk to other officers or to his headquarters. He can quickly call for assistance and send or receive vital information.

SPARKING SOUNDS

Connect a metal part of a steel file near the handle to a battery with a wire. You can do this with sticky tape. Connect another wire to the other terminal of the battery, and scrape the loose end of this wire along the file. See how small sparks fly. Place a radio nearby, turn it on and notice how noises come from the radio as the sparks occur. This is because the sparks send out short bursts of radio waves that the set picks up and turns into sounds. You may need to turn up the volume of the radio to hear them.

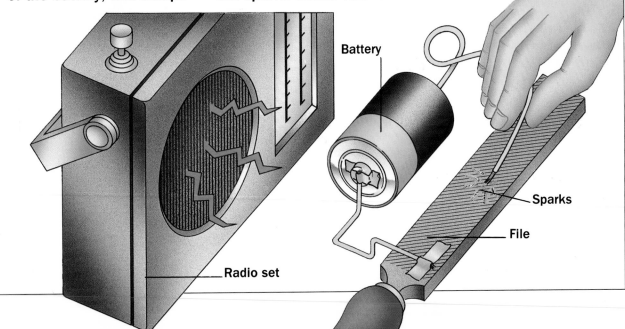

Battery

Sparks

File

Radio set

All methods of recording sound work by storing the electric signal from a microphone. There are two main methods: analog and digital. In analog recording, an exact copy of the sound wave is made, as on a record. In digital recording, the sound is stored as numbers, as it is on a compact disc.

STEREO SYSTEMS

Many homes have a stereo system, which may contain players for records, tapes and discs as well as a radio. The system also has an amplifier and a pair of loudspeakers to produce stereophonic (stereo) sound. Slightly different sounds come from each speaker, and this makes it sound as if the instruments and voices are spread out between the loudspeakers. There may also be a graphic equalizer, which can change the tone of the sounds, making low notes louder or softer, for example. The tape player in a stereo system can record sounds from discs or the radio.

TAPE PLAYERS

Tape players usually use cassettes, which contain reels of tape inside a plastic container. The reels turn to move the tape past a record/replay head in the player. The tape has a magnetic coating. When recording, an electric signal goes to a coil of wire in the head. The signal causes the coil to produce a magnetic field, which magnetizes the coating on part of the tape into a pattern called a track. On replay, the magnetic pattern on the tape produces an electric signal in the coil. This signal goes to an amplifier and loudspeakers, or earphones in a portable tape player. Music is recorded in two tracks along the tape to give stereophonic sound. The tape in fact has two pairs of tracks on it so that it can be turned over.

△ A stereo system can contain everything that you need for listening to all forms of recorded music.

▽ Cassettes usually contain tape for 60, 90 or 120 minutes of music, half of the time on each side.

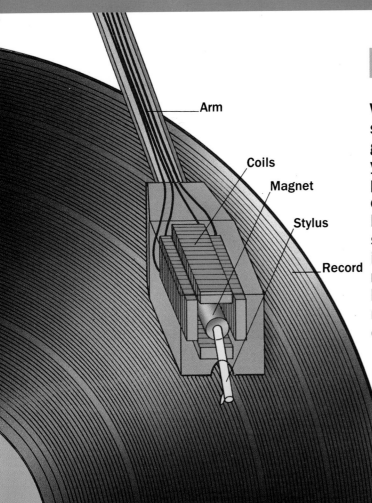

Arm

Coils

Magnet

Stylus

Record

RECORD PLAYERS

When a record is made, the electric signal goes to a machine that cuts a wavy groove in the surface of a disc. The record you buy is a plastic copy of this disc. The pick-up arm of the record player has a cartridge with a sharp stylus. This is lowered onto the spinning record, and the stylus vibrates as the groove moves past it. The stylus is connected to a small magnet that vibrates and is surrounded by coils of wire. The movement of the magnet sets up electric signals in the coils. These go to an amplifier.

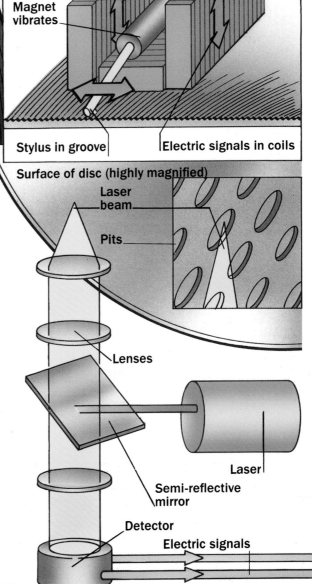

Magnet vibrates

Stylus in groove | Electric signals in coils

Surface of disc (highly magnified)

Laser beam

Pits

Lenses

Laser

Semi-reflective mirror

Detector

Electric signals

COMPACT DISCS

When a compact disc is made, the electric signal goes to a machine that cuts a spiral track containing millions of tiny pits in the surface of a disc. The disc you buy is a plastic copy of this disc. In a compact disc player, light from a small laser is aimed at the spinning disc. The beam is reflected by the surface. As the pits pass, the reflected beam flashes on and off. This beam goes to a detector that turns the light into an electric signal, and this signal goes to an amplifier.

A compact disc is a digital recording. This means that the vibrations of the sound wave are measured many thousands of times every second. Each measurement has a value, and the pits on the disc store this in the form of a coded number. Digital recording gives sound of very high quality.

People have known about sound and made music for thousands of years. Instruments have developed over many centuries. But it was little more than a hundred years ago that inventors began to build machines that could work with sound. These inventions have greatly advanced during this century.

Thomas Edison

Alexander Graham Bell

The telephone

Several people were involved in the invention of the telephone, but the credit is usually given to Alexander Graham Bell, who was born in Scotland and worked in the United States. Bell worked out how to change sound waves into an electric signal that would travel along a wire to a receiver, which would change the signal back into sound. In 1876, Bell was working on his invention when he spilt some acid and cried out to his assistant, "Mr Watson, please come here. I want you." Watson heard Bell's voice coming from the receiver — the first telephone message.

Sound recording

The famous American inventor Thomas Edison invented the phonograph, which was the first kind of record player, in 1877. Edison used a diaphragm connected to a needle, which was placed on a spinning cylinder of tinfoil. He spoke the nursery rhyme Mary Had a Little

Lamb, and the vibration of the diaphragm caused the needle to cut a groove into the tinfoil. Edison then placed the needle at the beginning of the groove and, as the cylinder spun, out came the sound of his voice from the diaphragm.

The record player uses the same principle to record sound. At first, recordings were made with wax cylinders. In 1887, Emile Berliner, a German engineer working in the United States, invented the gramophone, which used flat discs to record sound.

The principle of magnetic sound recording, which is used in tape players, was discovered in 1898 by the Danish engineer Valdemar Poulsen. He used wire instead of tape.

Heinrich Hertz

Radio

Radio waves were discovered in 1888 by the German scientist Heinrich Hertz. Only seven years later, the Italian engineer Guglielmo Marconi built the first radio set. It was used to transmit Morse code — not voices. Sounds were first sent by radio in 1906 by the Canadian engineer Reginald Fessenden.

Acoustic instrument
Any musical instrument that makes its own sounds and does not depend on electronics to produce sound.

Acoustics
The study of sound, especially the behaviour of sound waves in enclosed spaces such as concert halls.

Amplitude
The strength of a sound wave: loud sounds have a large amplitude. Sound-producing objects that vibrate over a greater distance give sounds with a larger amplitude.

Analog recording
A method of recording sound that stores a sound wave as a copy of the wave, such as the wavy groove on a record.

Compact disc
A record that uses digital recording. It consists of a rapidly spinning 12-centimetre disc with a spiral track of "dimples" that vary a beam of laser light to reproduce sounds.

Digital recording
A method of recording sound that stores a sound wave in the form of numbers that represent measurements of the wave.

Electrical signal
An electric current that changes in strength at the same frequency as a sound wave. It is an electrical copy of the sound wave, used in sound systems and electronic instruments.

Electronic instrument
A musical instrument that produces electrical signals, but no audible sound. The signals can be made audible through a sound system.

Frequency
The rate of vibration of a sound wave, measured in hertz (Hz), which equals the number of complete vibrations per second. Radio and other frequencies are also measured in hertz.

Molecules
The small particles of which most substances are made.

Pitch
The highness or lowness of a musical note, defined by the frequency or wavelength of its sound wave. Higher frequency and shorter wavelength give a higher pitch.

Sound wave
The form in which sound travels. A sound wave moves through a material such as air carrying vibrations from a vibrating object that is generating the sound. The object sets up alternate compressions and rarefactions in the air, which are regions of higher and lower pressure.

Speed of sound
Sound travels at a speed of 332 metres per second, which is equal to 1,194 kilometres per hour, in air at sea level. The speed of sound is slower high in the atmosphere, where the air is thinner and colder. Sound travels faster in liquids and solids than in air; it moves at about 1,500 metres per second in water and at 5,200 metres per second in steel.

Wavelength
The distance between two successive regions of high pressure (or low pressure) in a sound wave — the distance between the waves. A tuning fork sounding the note A with a frequency of 440 hertz produces sound with a wavelength of 77 centimetres.

Photographic Credits:
Cover and pages 14 both, 16, 17 bottom, 18, 22 and 25 both: Robert Harding Library; pages 5, 6 bottom, 8, 9, 12, 13 right, 19, 24 and 27: J. Allan Cash Library; pages 6 top, 10, 20 top and 28 top: Spectrum Colour Library; pages 7, 20 bottom and 26: Eye Ubiquitous; page 13 left: BMW Motors; pages 15 and 28 bottom: Roger Vlitos; page 30 top and middle: Popperfoto; page 30 bottom: Mary Evans Picture Library.